Before eatin
sit with your family.
Take turns flipping
the book to any page.
The page you land on,
is your message for
the day. Read it aloud.
You don't have to discuss
it. Just read it and pass
the book to the next person.
While you eat, you may want
to share how the message
connected to your day.
It is amazing how you
seem to flip to the page
you were meant to read that
day.

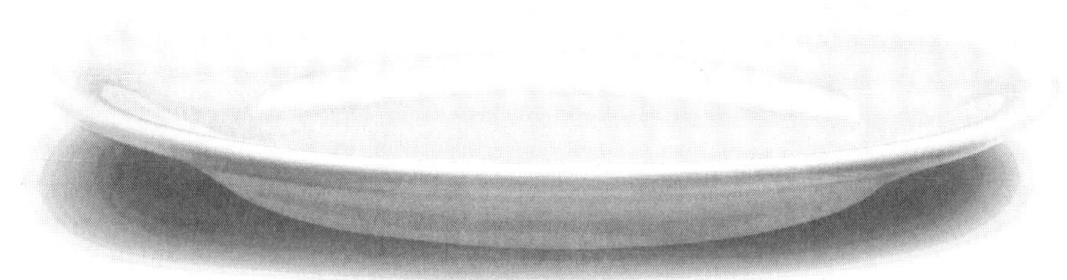

Challenge:

This part of the book is all about saying nice things to each other. Flip to a challenge page while you are waiting for dinner or after dinner! Some challenges are sincere and some are silly. The challenge is to make another person smile.

Kind words mean the most when they come from family.

Do a challenge while waiting for dinner. Or while eating dessert!

You can
do anything
in this life.

Challenge:

Tell the person on your right

something nice about their hair.

Take time
to enjoy
the little
things in
life.

Challenge:

Tell the person on your left

something nice they did today.

No matter what, there is always someone better than you. Keep practicing and stay positive.

Challenge:

Tell the person on your right

something they do that always makes you laugh.

Always
thank your
parents.
No matter how
old you are.

Challenge:

Tell the person on your left

how they are a leader in the family.

Don't be scared to show your creativity.

Challenge:

Tell the person in front of you

how much you love seeing them smile.

You can make someones day by giving them a compliment.

Challenge:

Tell the person in front of you

your favourite memory with them.

Take time
to enjoy life.
Work will
always be
there.

Challenge:

Tell the person on your left

that you appreciate them.

Take trips
that change
your life.
Trips that
make you
appreciate
home.

Challenge:

Tell the person on your right something nice about their outfit.

Your siblings care about you. You matter to them.

Challenge:

Tell the person who is in front of you that they should relax and you will do the dishes.

A simple
life is a
happy life.

Challenge:

Tell the person on your right

that you will make their lunch tomorrow.

You bring so much to our family. You are loved.

Challenge:

Tell the person on your left a joke. Make it a funny one.

You are someone's favourite person.

Challenge:

Tell the person on your right something nice about their socks.

Make sure
your life
is full of
happy
memories.

Challenge:

Tell the person on your left

how good they are at sports.

Blessings surround you.

Challenge:

Tell the person in front of you

they are amazing.

You bring leadership to your team. You are dedicated to your sport and a hard worker.

Challenge:

Tell the person on your right

that you like their face.

You can change a toxic environment. Be the good.

Challenge:

Keep smiling at **the person in front of you** until they notice.

You have a special gift with animals.

Challenge:

Tell the person on your right

that you love hearing their laugh.

You bring out the best in others.

Challenge:

Tell the person on your left

that after dinner you would like to have a push up contest.

Impossible.
Break the
word up and
it becomes
Im possible.

You can make
anything possible.

Challenge:

Ask the person in front of you

if they would like to play a game with you after dinner.

Have faith. Always have faith.

Faith in yourself and in others.

Challenge:

Start a game of telephone. Whisper something to **the person on your right.**

You are loved more than you you will ever know.

Challenge:

Tell the person in front of you something you like about their shirt.

Anyone can give up. It is the easiest thing to do. Show strength and determination instead.

Challenge:

Tell the chef

who made dinner.....

that it was the best meal you have ever had.

God will provide for you.

Find comfort in those words.

God will provide.

Challenge:

Ask the person on your right

what their favourite animal is?

Your smile, makes other people smile. Smile more often.

Challenge:

Ask the person on your left

where their dream vacation would be.

You were made for big things.

Don't give up. The future holds so many wonderful surprises.

Challenge:

After dinner draw a picture of the **person in front of you.**

You have
a kind
heart.

A heart that
loves and
forgives.

Challenge:

Tell the person on your right

what they are really talented at.

Never give up on your dreams.

You are the only person that can give up on them.

Challenge:

Tell the person on your left

that you love them but it is their turn to do dishes.

When in doubt... pray.

Pray for others.

Pray for yourself.

Challenge:

Tell the person on your right

a memory of when they were really kind to you.

Keep working hard and stay focused on your goal.

Challenge:

Tell the person on your left a book you think they would enjoy.

You are meant for big things in this life. Don't worry. It will happen.

Challenge:

Tell the person on your right

what you think they will be when they grow up.

Jesus will always be there for you.

Challenge:

Tell the person on your left

that they are your best friend.

Love your siblings. They will be your best friends one day.

Challenge:

Stare at the **person on your right** until they notice.

Your
mom and dad
think you
are perfect.

Challenge:

Tell the person on your left

that you will watch a movie with them.

No matter
where life takes
you, stay true
to yourself.

Always
stay
humble.

Challenge:

Tell the person in front of you

one of your favourite things about them.

Jesus believes
in you.

Your family
believes in you.
And your
friends
believe in you.

Challenge:

Tell the person on your right

that you will do their chores tomorrow.

You are valued and loved in this family.

Challenge:

Tell the person on your left

that they are really good at math and reading.

You have
a gift
to make
people
smile.

Challenge:

Tell the person in front of you....

that you really wish it was prime rib for dinner.

You give the best compliments.

Challenge:

Ask the chef what is for dessert?

You

have a

heart full

of gold.

Challenge:

Tell the person on the right

that you will make their lunch tomorrow.

You are
an angel
to many.

All your
help does not
go unnoticed.

Challenge:

Tell the person on your left

that you think they should wear blue tomorrow.

Be the teammate that others look up to.

Challenge:

Tell the person in front of you

that you love them.

Find the balance of fun and competitive.

Challenge:

Tell the person on your left

that you appreciate all they do for the family.

Someone
is praying
for you.

Challenge:

Tell the person on your right

that they are awesome.

Trust the process.

It is not easy.
But trust it.

Challenge:

Tell the person on your left

that you enjoy spending time with them.

God
is walking
along this
journey
with you.

Challenge:

Tell the person in front of you that you would like to have a thumb war with them after dinner.

You are loved.

Loved by friends.

Loved by family.

Challenge:

Ask the person on your right

what their favourite sport team is.

You are a miracle. This day is a miracle. Every breath we take is a miracle.

Challenge:

Tell the person on your left

what makes them a fun person.

You
deserve
good things
coming your
way.

Challenge:

Tell the person on your right that you enjoy being around them.

Something good happened today.

Challenge:

Tell the person in front of you

that you really like their style.

Always
search
for the
good.

Challenge:

Tell the person on your right

that they give the best high fives.

Always thank the chef. They cook with love.

Challenge:

Tell the person on your left

that you will make a treat for them this week.

Thank God for this day.

Challenge:

Ask the person in front of you

what their favourite song is.

It's okay
to know that
you are
the best at
something.
Just stay
be humble
about it.

Challenge:

Tell the person on your left

that they make you smile everyday.

You deserve
a holiday.
You have
been working
hard!

Challenge:

Tell the person in front of you

that you like their hair style.

When in doubt always show kindness.

Challenge:

Tell the person on your right

that they have a kind heart.

You are priceless.

Never forget that.

Challenge:

Tell the person on your left

that you are thankful for them.

Keep
dreaming
of how
you will
achieve
your goals.

Challenge:

Tell the person in front of you that you would like to pick out their outfit for tomorrow.

God knows
your
heart.

Challenge:

Tell the person on your right

something they are amazing at.

Always believe in something.

Challenge:

Ask the person in front of you

what concert they would love to go to.

Keep cheering on your family.

Challenge:

Ask the person on your right

what their dream car is.

Forgivness
will
set you
free.

Challenge:

Tell the person on the left that you really wish dinner would have been meatloaf.

You will always find strength in family and friends.

Challenge:

Tell the person in front of you

that you love hanging out with them.

Each new day brings an opportunity for happiness and love.

Challenge:

Tell the person on your right

that they are an awesome dancer.

Believe
in the
power of
prayer.

Challenge:

Tell the person on your left

that they are the favorite child and then giggle.

Your words hold a lot of power.

Challenge:

Tell the person in front of you

that they are smart.

Believe in miracles.

Believe in joy.

Believe in love.

Challenge:

Tell the person on your right

that you plan on living next to them when you are older.

Be happy. There is always something to be happy about.

Challenge:

Tell the person on your left

that you want to take a picture with them after dinner.

Trust God's plan.

All you have to do is trust.

Challenge:

Tell the person in front of you

what your favourite thing about them is.

You matter.

To God.
To family.
To friends.

Challenge:

Ask the person on your right

what their favorite pie is.

You have
a gift
of joy.
You make
other people
happy.

Challenge:

Ask the person on your left

if they will go for a walk with you after dinner.

Everything
is going
to work out.

Challenge:

Tell the person on your right

that you will help them with their homework.

God answers your prayers.

Challenge:

Tell the person on your left

that you will read them a book before bed.

Be proud of yourself.

Challenge:

Tell the person in front of you

that they have the best smile in the world.

Don't loose
your sparkle.
People love
your sparkle.

Challenge:

Tell the person on your right

that they do a good job brushing their teeth.

Learning to communicate is one of the most important tools to have.

Challenge:

Tell the person on your left

that you will make their bed for them in the morning.

You are important to your family.

Challenge:

Tell the person in front of you

that you wish dinner was brownies with ice cream.

You are strong. You can handle anything.

Challenge:

Tell the person on your left

that you love them.

Every day
smile at
a stranger.
It could
change their
day.

Challenge:

Tell the person on your left

that they are athletic and a hard worker.

Be the
best
part of
someones
day.

Challenge:

Tell the person on your right

never to give up on their dreams.

Do hard
things.

You really
can
DO HARD
THINGS.

Challenge:

Tell the person on your left

a funny story.

Live now
and not later.

Life is short.
Don't waste it.

Challenge:

Tell the person in front of you

that they make you happy.

Be positive. No one likes a negative person. Find a balance.

Challenge:

Tell the person on your right

that you are grateful for them.

Manners matter. Always be polite.

Challenge:

Tell the person on your left

that if you had a million dollars you would give it all to them.

Opinions
are great.
Share your
opinions.
Just don't
force your
opinions on
others.

Challenge:

Tell the person on your right that you think a perm would look nice in their hair.

Don't make big decisions until you have a calm heart.

Challenge:

Tell the person on your left

that you would like to borrow their shoes tomorrow.

Keep practicing. You will only get better.

Challenge:

Tell the person in front of you

that you think they are the best.

It is a
good
thing to
make
yourself
happy.

Challenge:

Tell the person on your right

a compliment.

You bring a lot of great things to our community.

Challenge:

Tell the person on your left

that you appreciate them.

Celebrate everyday.

Everyday is a gift.

Challenge:

Tell the person in front of you

that they bring FUN to the family.

It's okay
to let
go.

Challenge:

Tell the person on your left

that they are the best.

You

are worthy.

Challenge:

Start singing a song to the **person in front of you.**

You are in charge of your mindset.

Challenge:

Tell the person on your right

something they are really good at.

Don't be scared.
Take a risk.

Challenge:

Tell the person on your left

that you know big things are in their future.

Always
say
I love
you.

Challenge:

Tell the person on your right

that they deserve good things.

Thank
those who
inspire
you.

Challenge:

Tell the person on your left

that you wish you had their style.

You make
a difference
in your
coworkers
day.

Challenge:

Tell the person on your right

that they have nice handwriting.

Don't be scared to ask for help.

Challenge:

Tell the person in front of you

that you owe them a foot massage.

You are
loved by
all your friends
and family.

Challenge:

Tell the person on your left

that you think they are the coolest person in the world.

Tomorrow
brings
hope.

Challenge:

Tell the person on your left

that you think one day they will be famous.

Your creativity inspires others.

Challenge:

Tell the person in front of you that you would like to hang out with them after dinner.

Always donate. If you are lucky enough to buy new. Then donate the old.

Challenge:

Give everyone

at the table

a big hug.

Family
means
everything.

Manufactured by Amazon.ca
Acheson, AB